THE

DOOR OF HOPE

FOR

BRITAIN.

"Our help standeth in the name of the Lord, who made heaven and earth."

LONDON:
THOMAS BOSWORTH, 215, REGENT STREET.
1853.

In the interest of creating a more extensive selection of rare historical book reprints, we have chosen to reproduce this title even though it may possibly have occasional imperfections such as missing and blurred pages, missing text, poor pictures, markings, dark backgrounds and other reproduction issues beyond our control. Because this work is culturally important, we have made it available as a part of our commitment to protecting, preserving and promoting the world's literature. Thank you for your understanding.

THE
DOOR OF HOPE FOR BRITAIN.

They shall speak with the enemies in the gate.—Ps. cxxvii. 5.

A COSMOPOLITE cannot be a patriot. But each man should be a patriot. Christianity sanctifies all natural distinctions, be they personal, domestic, or national; yet it obliterates none. It prevents them from being the subjects of boasting, or the occasions of strife; yet it maintains their integrity. The ancients fought *pro aris et focis*. Christian nations have, or should have, but one altar. In the one House of God there should be no partition walls. Yet all nations, like all families, should have their *foci*; for even in the future dispensation shall be seen the "*nations* of the saved." King and country may be the idols of the narrow-minded. But to have neither is only the attainment of the infidel. That fraternity which abates all national quarrels is of Christ. But that which merges all national distinctions is of Antichrist. Under the garb of philanthropy, it at once effaces the landmarks, and bursts the bands, of Christ. It is, therefore, no mark of littleness, when Britons stand by Britain. It is our duty so to do. And we are not sinning against the rest of Christendom in preserving her integrity, provided the integrity of other nations be not sacrificed to her's.

God has no favorites among the nations. His ancient people were not His favorites. He did not choose them for their excellence. They grieved Him more than any. Nations do not rise or fall by chance. Their own efforts do not elevate, and those of others do not abase them. They are God's creatures and instruments. His dealings with them regard His purpose in Christ. Their place depends on the mission which He assigns to them, and their welfare on the faithfulness with which they fulfil it. Their polity is civil, but the argument of their being is ecclesiastical; for the Church is the mystery of Christ's kingdom on earth; and for that kingdom they prepare.

God has made Britain great. Not her constitution—nor her fleets and armies—nor her enterprise—nor her resources. These are the mere scaffolding. They are neither the building nor the builder. The condition of her greatness is that she fulfils the mission for which He made her great. Otherwise she must fall—tried, and found wanting. Wherein she has failed, the first conditions of her recovery are, knowledge of her errors; the honest, humble, and open confession of them; and the reform of her ways. Till these conditions are complied with, all expedients are in vain.

What has been her mission? And how has she fulfilled it?

Britain has a two-fold mission. She has one in common with other Christian nations. And she has one peculiar to herself. By both must her conduct be judged and her fate determined. And both concern her relation to the Church.

The history of one chosen people is the divine lesson for another. The Jews were chosen of God to be the depositaries of His truth, the examples of His ways, the ministers of His blessing, and the expectants of His kingdom. They were educated for a certain end—namely, to receive Messiah. They defeated the education—and so they missed the mark. They not only shed the blood of God; but they shed it by law. Their perverseness had gradually brought them into a false position, in which they could not, in conscience and consistency, do otherwise. God has turned to the Gentiles, not now to convert them all, but to take out of them a people for His name, in the place of that which He had lost. The Christian Church is indeed propagated by spiritual, instead of natural generation. Its standing, as the body of Christ, immeasurably transcends that of the most faithful or favored among the unbaptized. The end set before it is vastly more glorious. Yet the conditions of its salvation are similar to those under which Israel stood—namely, that it shall profit by the education of God, and be in all respects prepared to receive the Lord Jesus Christ, when He shall return, not in earthly but in heavenly glory, to reign on earth. All who defeat this education, shall also miss the mark. They shall crucify the Son of God afresh. They shall do it by law. They shall, through their sin, come into a position in which to do so shall seem the clear path of duty. That which will not be the temple of God, shall become a habitation of devils. They who will not be ruled by Christ, shall become the slaves of Antichrist. From this issue no amount of religious knowledge, of human wisdom or watchfulness, volition or exertion, can save them. God is the only Saviour; and He saves the obedient. To the disobedient, knowledge is the armoury, wisdom the counsel, and exertion the energy, of treason. By disobedience did man forfeit the first paradise—by it he shall fail of the second. Not the ignorance, but the disobedience of Christendom now hurries it to ruin. They who love pleasures more than God—not the votaries of sensual enjoyment, but they whose acts—pious or impious (the worse if the former),—are what they please to do, not what God would have them to do—they, being lawless, shall be gathered under the lawless one. They shall be judged according to their sin. For that true liberty which springs out of obedience, they shall have that bondage for which false liberty prepares. Our Christian standing, although a moral argument, is no physical charm, against apostasy. The perverse shall have strong delusion from God himself, to believe a lie. That lie shall be, in all its varied forms, the very thing which human aspirations shall hail, and human wisdom approve. And it shall be sealed by miracles which no scepticism can resist. "The day of Christ shall not come, except there come THE falling away first." The man of sin shall be revealed before the Man of righteousness—the son of perdition before the Son who abideth for ever—the usurper before the Heir—he that cometh in his own name before He that cometh in that of the Father—man, seeming to be God, before God really Man. It has ever been the way of God to make the apostasy of the faithless, the prelude of advancement to the faithful. The Christian apostasy, that which now ripens apace among us, agrees with the Jewish in this, that it shall be perfected ere men dream of their danger. But in this it differs, that while recovery from the Jewish is possible, recovery from the Christian is impossible; because the latter is a fall from the highest elevation of which man is capable.

Truly it is a thing to be wept over, not to be discussed in cold blood; to be feared by the trustful, not to be played with by the secure. *Antichristology*, in every form and sphere, is now becoming the small talk of European society. It is the wretched substitute for *Christology*, with those who know that they should be religious, yet like not to be godly—whose senses are no longer exercised to discern between good and evil—whose hearts will not follow the Lamb whithersoever He goeth. But the sole defence against the lie is progress in the truth; and the sole argument against it, that no lie is of the truth. Men may play with Antichrist as with a bird, and bind him for their maidens, and make a covenant with him, yea take him for their servant as they please. Satan will laugh while he lets them play; he will furnish them with more playthings; he will let them bind him, and thus more surely take them in his snare. The study of evil shall never save us from it. We shall thus only the sooner learn to accept it. But, looking at Christ, and abiding in Him, by this token shall we conquer—"Greater is He that is in us than he that is in the world."

Now, if such be the turning point in the destiny of the Church, we should expect to find the same in that of Christian nations. To talk of separating religion from politics, argues the profoundest ignorance of what religion and politics are. Blended they should not be. The State has no right to dictate the doctrine and discipline or to perform the functions of the Church. And, despite the sophism of Thomas Aquinas, that, because Moses called the Jews a "priestly kingdom," and Peter called Christians "royal priests," therefore, as kings had temporal rule under the law, so have priests under the Gospel, it is equally clear that the priest has no more right to political than to domestic functions. But the Church should furnish all her children with right principles of action for every sphere of life, and therefore for the exercise of civil government, as the most important sphere of all. No actions of Christian men, and especially no actions of Christian rulers, can be indifferent before God, either in character or in consequences. They should be accordant with His will, as learned in the Church. In so far as they are, the nations please Him. In so far as they are not, the reverse. Therefore if the destiny of the Church depends on obedience to Him, that of Christian nations no less does so. And if the Church is, through lawlessness, in danger of falling under the lawless one, the nations are so too. In this only do the cases differ, that, while the judgment on the Church shall be ecclesiastical, that on the nations shall be national.

Hence, what we have now to fear is, that the nations of Christendom, being found unfaithful to God in their civil polity, whether by despising His precepts, by favoring evil, or by hindering good, shall be carried away by a vast political delusion, the counterpart of the ecclesiastical, and thus fall under the political domination of Antichrist. We have no warrant to look for the exemption of any nation from this fate, save as the reward of fidelity to Christ. And, as in Church, so in State, apostasy shall be the rule—fidelity the rare exception.

Of this sad consummation we have, in the prophetic portions of holy Scripture, many intimations, diversified in form, but alike in substance. And the events of the first French Revolution, coupled with the career of the first

Napoleon, were a dim foreshowing of it, to which few thoughtful men, political or religious, have been blind. That crisis has passed away. But the greater crisis which it foreshowed is yet before us. Britain was not only exempted from the former in a way too manifest to be regarded as accidental, but prominently used by God in bringing it to an end. And it is for us a practical question of the most vital importance; whether we may hope to see her in like manner both exempted from the latter, and used in bringing it also to an end?

The sins of Britain have not been small. And the amount of her privileges and blessings has greatly aggravated them. Although she has, alas! added many (perhaps the worst) to the catalogue of her sins since Napoleon's fall, they were already manifest enough before his rise, to justify her then sharing the fate of the rest of Europe. And we can ascribe her exemption only to one or both of two causes—viz., that, in spite of her many provocations, she did peculiarly give national witness for God against the delusions and wickedness of the time; and that God, who useth whom He will, had other and ulterior work in store for her, which required that she should be then exempted. We shall see the truth of both reasons.

At the time of the first French Revolution Britain was unquestionably the land where apostolic institutions, elsewhere either retained to be abused or purged almost into evanescence, were found to the greatest extent at once comparatively intact and comparatively pure — where the pulse of manly freedom beat most highly in the veins of men who bowed to the majesty of law—where the *liberty* of the *subject* was a formula realized in both its factors—where religion had the largest place and the firmest root in the family, the school, the market, the tribunal, the senate, and the court; in fine, where the habits and institutions of the people still pre-eminently gave that honour to God which He could requite with honour.

It seemed as if, in that dark passage of our history, the Commonwealth and the Protectorate, Britain had anticipated the fate of other lands, in order to be afterwards justly exempted from it, and be a ready instrument for a peculiar work. With all the fanaticism or hypocrisy of the Roundheads, their principles are as little to be compared with the blasphemies of revolutionary France, as the North American with the French Republic. Our constitutional liberty and earnest piety have both outlived their sad metamorphosis in the 17th century. The chaos of the French Revolution, and the fixation which succeeded it, were not permitted to affect us. Our bulwarks were loyalty and religion. Those who, in Britain, called the evil good, were but like heretics, who make the faithful manifest. While the rest of Europe was beguiled, bewildered, or intimidated, the mass of this nation neither wavered in judgment nor faltered in action. From the first, we took our stand to contradict, and our measures to abate, the lie. We would not believe them who said they were in sport, while they "cast firebrands, arrows, and death." We held no parley with the criminals. We threw down the gauntlet for truth on the battle field of national rights. We fought neither from malice nor for conquest. We vindicated the well being of society. And when God would break the rod with which He had chastised the sins of His heritage, He broke it by those, who, while they justified His wrath, saw and testified that the rod itself was the power of Satan. For almost the first time in the history of the world, a war was waged, holy in its origin, just in its conduct, and sanctifying in its effects; a war of *liberation* from more than a human oppressor. The spontaneous eucharists of the victors in Leipzig's great battle of nations, were no *Te Deum* pomp of state hypocrisy and triumphant wrong. And, whether Blucher saved or seconded our great departed captain, the day of Waterloo saw Britain and Prussia elevated in common, under the eye of God, to the peerless honour of throwing back the onset, and scattering the power of that day's Antichrist, when loosed, like Satan, for a season. An omen, this, perhaps, of fellowship in yet higher things to come. So did God at that time pardon those whom He spared, and employ those who would serve Him.

But how stands it now? The nations have forgotten their vows of penitent thankfulness. They have returned to their folly. They are leprous again. The pent up lava of the volcano has wrought wider destruction in the earthquake. God has once more shaken the nations into chaos, and made drastic medicine their bread. We have seen the beginnings of what an ancient foresaw, αἱ δημοκρατιαι αἱ μελλουσαι γιγνεσθαι. And we have been once more exempt! Whence is this? What does it indicate? What hopes does it warrant?

In God's patience, the end is not yet. He has stayed the wrath. But have men changed their ways? Alas! far less than before. In the counsels and decrees of the Allied Powers after the fall of Napoleon we find a public faith in God—a purpose, however inadequately fulfilled, to serve Him—a regard at last to the good of the subject—an amendment of national life, which we now look for, comparatively, in vain. The so-called friends of order—they who would conserve—are now as godless as they who would change and destroy. Reaction, grovelling and selfish, cowardly and faithless, impenitent and infatuated, too dishonest to confess the sin and untruth of its base concessions, and bold only when secure, has no higher thought than to restore the *status quo*, by fair means or by foul. According to the words of Burke, " Kings have become tyrants from policy, because their subjects are rebels on principle," and the little finger of the son is made thicker than the father's loins. Nought is to be seen but potsherd with potsherd in ignoble strife. Flesh overreaches, coerces, exterminates flesh. Bullets and eaves-droppers keep the peace of incarcerated manhood. Every new measure turns a fresh ward of the lock and gives a fresh twist to the rope. But all in vain. Satan is thus to be neither banished nor bound. The cup of retribution is only filled to the brim. When the winds and waves of revolution arose, every house shook, for lack of God's cement. The stout-hearted were as women—their faces gathering blackness—their hearts failing—their hands on their loins, as in travail. When the beast arose, the mighty were afraid. They were cast down at the sight of him. They hastened to stroke him the right way of the hair, and give him what he would. Archbishops blessed trees of liberty. Preachers canonized its martyrs. The dogs that could not bark learned to whine out flattery. The false prophets sanctified the delusion and sin of the rulers. But these made no peace with God. Now that they have found breathing time again, they say: "We were once surprised; we shall not be so again." But what if God watch for the evil? They say: "Our hosts shall save us." But who shall keep the hosts? "Great hosts save not a king." What if Satan leaven, or the blast of God scatter the hosts? They say: "Our mountain stands strong." But what if God touch the mountain?

Meanwhile, not by the will of God, but by the stealth of Satan, a new form of order does arise—the worse for being religious in its accidents—satanic in its essence. By a magic paradox, only the more strange that it surprizes none whom it transmutes, the blossoms of revolution bear the fruit of empire. To ηθος το αυτο, και αμφω δεσποτικα των βελτιονων. "The grace of God and the will of the people" have brought forth, from the kettle of the sorcerer, one, who neither seeks the one nor obeys the other, but will use that popular will, which he dictates, as a divine dispensation for crime. And selfish reactionists stupidly hail him as a godsend, tender to him unasked the hand of brotherhood, nay give him *carte blanche* to do what he lists—merely because he can rule. Whether by God or by Satan matters not to them. Thus, as of old in Herod and Pilate, do the most diverse forms of flesh betray their common basis. Alas! how wide of even the heathen's description: ὁ μεν βασιλευς νομιμος, ὁ δε αρχων ακολουθος, ὁ δε αρχομενος ελευθερος, ἁ δε ὁλα κοινωνια ευδαιμων. The dragon and the beast have two forms indeed, but one evil heart. And the words of the false prophet to that one heart, are carried out alike in the diverse works of both.

But how does Britain stand? Shall we too be deceived? or, being not deceived, shall we be overwhelmed?

If we are not deceived, we cannot be overwhelmed. The way of God is certain salvation. The judgment and the sin judged are ever correlatives. Salvation and destruction come only on those who are beforehand prepared for them. If we do not believe a lie—we need not fear it.

But shall we escape the great coming delusion? We know it to be a canon of the Divine procedure, that God not only has at all times a refuge for His truth, but exhibits salvation parallel with destruction, on the same theatre, and in the same measure. And although we cannot conclude with certainty, we may justly infer, that those whom He has exempted from the beginnings and the progress of judgment, are those also whom He especially desires to exempt from its further stages and consummation. Judgment, in this dispensation, is not confined to mere corporeal or temporal suffering; for the worst judgment of all is the blindness and impenitence of the prosperous. And there is good ground to believe that we shall now see the wicked prosper, as they have never done before. Nay, this fact may form a large element in the machinery by which men will be deluded. Yet the temporal calamity of nations may be both a token and an accessory of spiritual. And, if there is anything in the corporate instinctive presentiments of a nation, if " coming events cast their shadows before," there is not a little in the present tone of public feeling in Britain to fill the thoughtful with concern. As high looks go before a fall, so is the loud cry of peace and safety too often the prelude of judgment and the companion of latent alarm. Our affairs, in their mere human aspect, have seldom been more prosperous. Peace and enterprise abroad—flourishing trade and manufactures at home—poverty diminished —the troubles of disturbed interests quieted— the coffers of the state more than filled— yet withal, an undefined uneasiness, which will not be comforted away—the sign that in the Divine aspect of our affairs there is a controversy unsettled between us and God. The tempestive death of an octogenarian we regard, in spite of ourselves, as a signature of the time. We say that his mantle must have fallen on others. Yet we doubt it much. As, at the time when a prophet of our day rang the knell of Babylon, our levity turned the burden of the Lord against us into the key note of a musical festival, so did God thus order it, that at the obsequies of our aged hero, we appropriated to ourselves, for music's sake, those ominous words of Isaiah, which describe a people deserted by God, and which warn us to cease from man, when the Lord arises to shake terribly the earth. Do not our public words of stoutness betray, while they cloak, the misgivings of our hearts! What means it, that in one breath we are assured of halcyon peace and incited to busy armament? Whence this reefing the canvass for a storm, with not a cloud in the sky? Whence this fear of invasion, without a quarrel or a threat? Whence this craven invitation of evil—this fascinated consent to the power of a spell—this tacit anticipation of a day—

"When Seine shall swallow Tiber; and the Thames,
"By letting in them both, pollute her streams."
(HERBERT.)

Whence is this? The true answer is short—*Britain's conscience is not clean.*

It is written—"When these things begin to come to pass, then look up, and lift up your heads; for your redemption draweth nigh." How do we interpret the phenomena of the time? Have we the key to the riddle of the future? Have we a beacon which lights across the chasm? Do we know and hail the issue? Or do we grope in the dark, and shrink as from a precipice? Are we surprised or prepared? Are we passing into darkness, or emerging into light? Do we fast or feast because of what is coming? Do the things, which fill others with fear, fill us with hope? Or do we still fear their fear? Here lies the touchstone of our condition. If the Lord is not our fear, He cannot be our sanctuary. If He has a controversy with us, He cannot be our fear; for His is the fear of sons, not of slaves or enemies. There is no profit in croaking. There is no kindness in disheartening. There is no patriotism in despondency. But to remove all mistake as to the nature of the question at issue is the best of all services. We have to do with God. If He be for us, who shall be against us? But if He be against us, who shall stand against Him? Let Britons be of what stuff they may;—what shall avail the prestige of our name—what the heart of our masses—the bottom of our troops—the range of our rifles—the list of our first-rates—the screws of our steamers? These are all things which we do well to look to—things which God can use on our behalf. But what if He will not use them? Are they our gods, that we should trust them still? Can we stem the tide of His disfavour? Have we not rather to fear, for our long spared island, calamity the most improbable, perhaps the most sudden? There is a godless dread which faith cannot share in; but there is a godly dread which faith should experience. There is a godless confidence which faith cannot feel; but there is a godly confidence which faith should inspire. The godly dread warns us to repent. The godly confidence is the proof that we have done so. Have we this proof or no?

So much for our history and prospects in the position common to us with other Christian nations. But we should understand neither our sin nor our duty, neither our danger nor our hope, if we did not advert to that which is peculiar in the place and mission of our country. This peculiarity rests partly on scriptural intimations, partly on facts.

The parallel drawn by many expositors between ancient Tyre and Great Britain, is not without some foundation in truth, or destitute of instruction for us. It consists of five parts—referring to the position—to the sin—to the judgment—to the service—and to the blessing of that famous city.

Tyre—a stronghold in the days of Joshua and those of David,—honoured to aid in the building of the temple under Solomon, and in its rebuilding under Ezra, was the greatest emporium of oriental trade; much sought unto, yet no less envied, and destroyed, first by Nebuchadnezzar, then, after seventy years, by Alexander. Isaiah calls it " the joyous city, whose antiquity is of ancient days," "the merchant city, with strongholds," "the crowning city, whose merchants are princes, whose traffickers are the honourable of the earth." Isaiah xxiii. And Ezekiel calls it, "the abode of seafaring men, the renowned city, strong in the sea, whose terror was upon all that haunted it, situate at the entrance of the sea, a merchant of the people for many isles, whose borders were in the midst of the seas—who was replenished and made very glorious in the midst thereof—who filled many people and enriched the kings of the earth with the multitude of her riches—whose builders had perfected her beauty—and whose prince, full of wisdom and perfect in beauty, sealed up the sum, and was the anointed cherub that covered, in the midst of the stones of fire." Ezek. xxvi. to xxviii.

The sin of this city lay chiefly in its usurpation of the place of Jerusalem, in its pride, and in its harlotry. The Lord declared by Ezekiel that He was against Tyre, because she had rejoiced in the breaking of Jerusalem, which had been the gates of the people, and in her own replenishment by the laying waste of that theocratic metropolis of the earth. Ezek. xxvi. 2.

As to the king of Tyrus, He declared that, his heart being lifted up because of his riches and his beauty, and his sanctuaries being defiled by the iniquity of his traffic, he had set his heart as the heart of God, and said, "I am a god, I sit in the seat of God, in the midst of the seas." Ezek. xxviii. 2, &c. And Isaiah announced, that after Tyre should have lain desolate and been forgotten for a time, she should again turn to her hire, court her lovers with many songs, and commit fornication with all the kingdoms of the world. Is. xxiii. 15, &c. These three sins bear a most striking analogy to those ascribed, both in the Prophets and in the Apocalypse, to Babylon, as the abode of God's captive people, as the land whose kings were the autocrats of the world—as the city which made all the earth drunken.

The judgment wrought on Tyre, was in terms of its sin, and still more remarkably akin to that on Babylon. It became "the destroyed in the midst of the seas." Once a fortress of strength, it was levelled with the ground. The sea, from which Tyre had thriven, and in which it had gloried, was (as with Babylon) made the instrument of its overthrow. Once adorned to the full, it was made bare like the top of a rock. Once full of music, it was consigned to silence. Once the joy of the earth, it was made a terror. The report of its overthrow was like to the report of Egypt's plagues. The professed object of the judgment was to stain the pride of all glory. Hence, at the fall of Tyre, as at that of Babylon, all nations lamented, kings looked on amazed, and the earth was moved. And the king of Tyre, being man, and not God, in the hand of him that slew him, was destroyed from the midst of the stones of fire, and made a terror, as Tyre itself, to all.

But there was a blessing in store for Tyre, of which we read no counterpart for Babylon. Not only was Hiram honoured to aid in the building of the temple, under Solomon, the Prince of Peace, but the daughter of Tyre should be there with a gift, when Jesus, the true King of glory, should return to the marriage, Ps. xlv.; and after Tyre should have disclosed her harlotry, her merchandise should be for them that dwelt before the Lord. Is. xxiii.

Now what has been the character of Britain? Are not the features of Tyre seen literally in her social position among the nations; and are they not also spiritually fulfilled in the religious influence to which her social position has introduced her? Do not all nations take their tone from her in social progress? Do they not frequent her marts, replenishing her, and replenished by her in turn? Does not her merchant-fleet cover the farthest seas? Does not her enterprize awaken the dormant capabilities of every clime! Has she not made science and trade useful and honourable? Has she not been the bulwark of constitutional liberty, the land where men breathe freely and live secure? Does not her constitution embrace in wholesome combination elements elsewhere at strife? Has it not been the wonder and envy of the world; that which all well meant political efforts instinctively imitate? Is she not, with all her faults, the land of practical godliness, and large philanthropy. Has she not done more to civilize the world, than any other nation, Greece and Rome not excepted?

But, on the other hand, has she not confounded the body of Christ with the body politic, by forgetting the place, and usurping the office of the Catholic Church? Has not the religious badge of her children been "Briton" not

"Christian?" And, separated from the major part and the mightiest ordinances of the Church of God, has she not reconciled herself to the evils of schism, by sounding the praises of her own Articles, Liturgy, and Succession? Where are her tears over the lacerated Church of God? Where her sense of its palsied weakness? Has she not rather imagined that Britain and the Bible can do all for the world which the Church Catholic and her ordinances could? As Tyre said, "Jerusalem is turned unto me;" has not Britain said, "The Church of God is the British empire;" a light sin this in the eyes of man, but not light in those of God; a state of things, which, while it does indicate, totally misrepresents, the true national office which Britain should, and through God's mercy shall, have? Moreover, is not Britain, κατ ἐξοχην, the land of pride, both national and personal; fondly deeming herself superior to all, because elevated higher; now an offence and now a laughing-stock to Europe, through her insular sauciness; cursed by those whom she helps; spurned by those whom she leads; the bully of the nations, provoking a thrashing, and on the high road to get it? And are we as exempt from the principles of Antichrist, as we have been hitherto exempt from his judgment? While Germans set themselves as God in daring philosophical speculation, and Frenchmen in reckless political change, do not we set ourselves as gods in the use of the creature for the service of man? Are there not heard among us the boastings of Antichrist, in our form of utterance, as plainly as with them in theirs? Are not the "inspirations" of the Crystal Palace as much a mockery of the name and Spirit of Christ as the second Pentecost of Young Germany, or the second Incarnation of Young France? Is not the transmutation of religious ordinances into Acts of Parliament as profane as their prostitution on the marketplace of intellect? And may not Britain be yet seduced to sell her soul to Antichrist for the maintenance or recovery of her high place among the nations? These are questions worth answering.

What then has Britain to fear at the hand of God? That, having corrupted her ways, she shall be put to shame on the very theatre of her glory—that God will read a lesson to the nations by her fall, by her emptying and utter desertion—that the nations shall bring her down, trample her under foot, and then involve her in their own ruin—perhaps by outward force—perhaps by a leaven pervading her internal being—perhaps by both. What is wrought elsewhere by violence, may with us pass through the legitimate forms of Parliament. But the thing done shall be the same.

On the other hand, what has Britain to hope? We have already seen how each of the nations might, by avoiding their common sin, have escaped their common judgment. We have also seen, how Britain, by her avoidance of the sin, did escape the judgment, in that measure in which the sin and the judgment were at the time developed. But England has at the present crisis, as distinguished from the past, a calling peculiar to herself. Her exemption from the approaching plenitude of judgment, will depend not merely on her fidelity to the grace which the nations have hitherto enjoyed in common, but on her fidelity to that larger measure and peculiar form of grace which she is now chosen to receive, in order that she may aid other Christian nations in resisting the most subtle and intense of all temptations—the claims of

Antichrist, as the rival of Christ in his threefold character of prophet, priest, and king.

The prophetic announcements of God, be they threatenings or promises, are not the words of a fortune-teller. And we may not use them as if we were consulting one. They are not given to feed curiosity, to seal despondency, or to sustain presumption, by the unalterable oracles of a fate; or to violate the order of nature by turning the future into plain history. The purposes of God are as unchangeable as Himself. But they are not the less unchangeable, that His dealings towards men and nations not only change but often are reversed, with the change or reversal of the course followed by those whom these dealings regard. Indeed, they could not be His dealings, if they did otherwise; for they should cease to be the dealings of a moral Governor, of a just and merciful Father. He announced to Nineveh not only the event but the date of its destruction. Yet the threatening and the date were both falsified. And why? Because the city against which the threat was uttered became no longer that on which it could be executed. Be the words as absolute as they may, their unconditional fulfilment is impossible. They should thus cease to be a moral warning. As there is no blessing, so there is no judgment, save to those who are found worthy of it when it comes.

Grant then, that Britain, like Tyre of old, is met at every turn by declarations of judgment, there is no necessity that it should touch her. There is no reason why she should not escape it. If she is no longer the Britain threatened, she shall not be the Britain judged. Let us not be spell-bound by the threatenings of God, as by the decree of a fate. Let us rather rouse ourselves to obviate them all, by putting that away which calls them forth. By this we shall please Him. It is not His will to vindicate His truth by our ruin. He would rather seem false, if we may be saved. Should we not be as jealous for the truth of His promises, as for that of His threatenings? And are not His recent acts in this land the mightiest argument for the former—a living proof that His mercy endureth for ever?

The destruction of the king of Tyre, from among the stones of fire, points to the perversion of the very highest spiritual privileges.

But whether the application of this type to Britain be legitimate or not, Holy Scripture affords abundant warrant to expect an advancement of the Church to a spiritual perfection corresponding to the spiritual evil now approaching its full development. "When the enemy shall come in like a flood, the Spirit of the Lord shall lift up a standard against him." A Church without rent or blemish, pure and adorned, is the only true bride of the Lamb. To prove that this shall be, we need not dwell on arguments. We can point to facts. And these facts are found in Britain.

When John the Baptist prepared the way of the Lord, he was declared to be more than a prophet; because he was the *preparer*. At no period of the Christian dispensation have prophets been wanting, who formed pictures of hope and spake words of faith, not only concerning the return of our risen Lord, but also concerning the transmutation of the Church, as a temple to which, from its condition, He could not come, into one to which He could. In this particular Britain has not been singular. In her, as elsewhere, have such thoughts and hopes been often revived only to perish with the holy persons who entertained them. But in another respect she has been singular. A Christian *preparer* has (to use the scriptural figure) been raised up in her, to take up and realize the transient visions of the prophets, and to direct the eyes of men to that quarter in which, and that instrumentality by which, God is about to form Christ again in His people, and to restore His temple for the reception of the returning Saviour. In this land especially was a cry, ignorant indeed, yet faithful and united, raised by the contrite, that God would *stir up His power* and come to save us. In this land *first* did He do so. This land first rang with the tidings of His mercy, with the alarm of the trumpet against both the strongholds of bondage and the palaces of lukewarm repose. In this land first did the Spirit of Christ once more break His well nigh perennial silence, manifest His forgotten presence, fill our mouth with laughter, and our tongue with singing, and scatter with His light both the darkness and the slumbers of the night, before the day-star arising in our hearts. In this land first did God put to His hand the second time, to rebuild His altar and order the sacrifices thereon

—to repair what man had forfeited—to purify what man had defiled—to bring cosmos out of chaos—condescending to the low estate of His people that He might lift them up for ever, settling us on the ancient foundations, building us up in the same faith and fellowship as at the first, gathering the wanderers, comforting the desolate, giving sight to the blind, hearing to the deaf, walking to the lame, cleansing to the lepers, life to the dead, gently accustoming the wounded, wasted, enfeebled body to the food and functions of health. In this land first have the gifts of the Spirit—elsewhere, through lack of culture and guidance, like water spilt upon the ground—been turned, in the congregations of the faithful, to their true use of edifying. In this land first has the eschatology of the Church been rescued out of the theories of disobedient dreamers, and employed in the discipline of obedient children. In this land first has the prediction of our Lord's return been received as a living promise on behalf of the whole Church—a hope for which to labour and by which to purify—a catholic hope embodied in catholic congregations who are actually and rapidly going on to perfection in catholic worship and holy works, serving the living and true God and waiting for His Son from heaven, our deliverer from the wrath to come.

In this land *alone* has God called, and by much wonderful discipline trained, the elders of His universal Church, by whom Jesus, the great Angel of the Covenant, may bind together, bless, and guide her, edifying her unto the measure of the stature of His fulness. In it alone has He aided the weakness, assured the faith, and enlightened the understanding of His people, by constructing, as it were, a microcosm, in which to exhibit the manner of His perfect worship and service, for a pattern to all the baptized, τα αισθητως ιερα των νοητων απεικονισματα, και επ' όντα χειραγωγια και ὁδος. In this land alone has He appointed a centre, not the throne of earthly empire, or the chair of exaggerated episcopate, but the seat of Apostles, as Jerusalem of old, from which shall go forth His power and law, and in the unity of which, the Catholic Church shall find both symbol and basis for her own. The things which have burst upon Europe with resistless surprise are the very things which God has foreshowed, in this land, to those who would hear His word, who like Abraham, have been

His friends, and who alone, forewarned and thus forearmed, are not overtaken as by a thief. From this land alone has the voice of mercy, the work of restoration, the plerophory of blessing gone forth. And as, in the beginning, the seal of Apostleship was found in the Churches which Apostles builded, so is the seal of this work, at the end of the age, to be found in the European Churches—in the baptized, out of every land and communion, made alive to their baptismal unity and privileges—in the lost sheep gathered into folds—in the faithful led on towards perfection, with a speed which astonishes themselves—in the change from death to life, from darkness to light, from doubt to certainty—from despair to hope, from discontent to patience, from trouble to peace, from confusion to order, from falsehood to truth, from hatred to love—from infidelity, on the one hand, and schism on the other, to the real catholicity of faith—from the uniformity of death to the unity of life. For the first time since the Apostolic Age does Christendom now contain in its bosom government truly œcumenic, worshippers and worship truly catholic, Christians really needing and using all others as members of a body, believers soberly expecting to see the Lord, and occupying till He come,—living examples, in part, of what should pervade the whole—not a new piece on an old garment, or new wine in old bottles, but both new—not a heterogeneous element injected to fester all around it, but a healing begun in some members, that it may extend to the rest by the legitimate circulation of a common life—not the predominance of one section to the extinction of the rest, or the introduction of novel conceits in contempt of things existing,—but the due recognition, selection, adjustment, and fuller development of all that has been or is of God, in any part of His Church. In this phenomenon lies the divine panacea for the evils of our age; not the false, and, even though true, idle *dogma* of the blessed Virgin's immaculate conception, but the *divine fact* now appearing and yet to be fully seen—that holy virgin, the Church of God, pregnant with the future glory of Christ in His saints—that Queen, whose children shall be instead of her fathers, whose name, more than Mary's, shall be remembered in all generations, and who shall be praised for ever, by the people, for an achievement of faith, analogous to, yet transcending, her's. (Ps. xlv.) This work is the banner given to them that fear God. In Britain has this banner been displayed. In all this Britain is the honoured agent. God has used her to lead the way. We may not, indeed, confound Britain with the Church in Britain, by transferring to the former conclusions belonging to the latter. And we surely believe, that, to be taken out of this world and caught up to meet the Lord in the air, will be the only ultimate escape from the things that are coming both on the earth and on all that prefer abode on earth to citizenship in heaven. But it is consistent with the whole analogy of God's dealings to believe that, till that time arrive, He will not leave His people without a local refuge on earth, that He will not arbitrarily change the site of that refuge, and that the nation which has been the cradle of His grace, and which is yet the central theatre of His working, the fulcrum, so to speak, or που στω of His power, shall not share the fate of others, if it be faithful to this its pre-eminent calling.

Here then lies the true turning point of Britain's destiny. Does she acknowledge or ignore this act of God? Does she welcome and cherish, or does she dislike, and would she expel, that which He has established in the heart of her body politic? Does she prefer, or not, her unsupported, chemically resolved episcopacy, or her Church by grace of Parliament, to this perfect way of God? Does she hasten or delay to accept the blessing of the latter? Does she honestly and thankfully confess its source? Is she, or would she, gladly be pervaded by its virtue? Does she, or will she, as a nation, live and move, devise and determine, act and suffer, for its sake? Will she use her best legitimate influence to recommend it to other nations; and renounce, if need be, for its sake, her national interests and pre-eminence? Or, in this day when God shall be known in His holy habitation as the Father of the fatherless and the Judge of the widows, will she cast in her lot with those nations which decree unrighteous decrees, to make widows their prey, rob the fatherless, turn aside the right of the needy, and thus call down His judgment? Such are the questions which she must ask and answer; for on her practical answer to these, and not on the changes of politics, the currents of trade, or the chances of war, does it depend, whether God, who has hitherto so signally saved her, will now reject her, or whether He will honour her now more highly than ever, and identify her cause with His, because she counts that which He has planted within her, not only the hope of the Church and the health of the world, but the palladium of her own national being.

If she follow the better alternative, she has nothing to fear. They who come up against her shall return as they came. The vessel of her state shall bound over every billow, as the ark did in the days of old. The wings of the Assyrian may darken all Immanuel's land. But there shall be light in her tabernacles. The flood may reach to the neck. But the Head, and they who hold by Him, through joints and bands of His appointment, shall not be submerged. That day, in which God cuts off from Babylon the *name* and *remnant* and *son* and *nephew*, in which He breaks the Assyrian in His land and treads him under foot on His mountains (Is. xiv. 22), shall be the day of our national redemption. And God shall have His elected one among the nations, as well as His undefiled one among the Churches. This nation shall be the handmaid of the Church, the helper of other lands. And her merchandize, no longer the substitute for spiritual grace, or the hire of national harlotry, shall find its true employment in the service of the redeemed.

In this, man's transition state, still bearing a curse removed, already tasting a blessing unrevealed, it is idle to ask, and presumptuous to dictate, in what measure, on any given occasion, we are to be exempt from the former and partakers of the latter. This we must humbly refer to Him who mingleth mercy with judgment. We may neither seek to evade the chastisement of sons, nor appropriate the fate of enemies. If we suffer, we are judged of the Lord, that we may not perish with the wicked. But, if we will judge ourselves, we shall not be judged. If we are to fall, let us fall into the hands of the Lord, not into those of men. The axe has no mercy. The hewer has. But we need not fall. If the living will seek no longer to the dead, but to their God, He shall be their sanctuary. No weapon formed against them shall prosper; and from Him who dwelleth in Zion shall they be for signs and for wonders.

LONDON:
G. J. PALMER, SAVOY STREET, STRAND.

Works

JUST PUBLISHED.

THE HISTORY OF THE CHRISTIAN CHURCH. Vol. I. The Church in the Apostolic Age. By HENRY W. J. THIERSCH, Doctor of Philosophy and Theology. Translated from the German by Thomas Carlyle, Esq., the Scottish Bar. 12mo., cloth, 6s.

"In his earlier works Dr. Thiersch had shown powers of no ordinary kind; sound scholarship, a reverential tone of mind, a just and discriminating appreciation of doctrines and principles, a candid spirit and a clear style. * * * * *
* * His History of the 'Church in the Apostolic Age,' which appeared in Germany in the early part of this year, is the first division of a larger work on 'The Ancient Christian Church,' and I earnestly hope that it will be translated into English, for it is not only a learned but instructive work."—*Rev. T. K. Arnold, in the Theological Critic.*

THE REVIVAL OF THE FRENCH EMPERORSHIP. Anticipated from the Necessity of Prophecy. By the Rev. GEORGE STANLEY FABER, B.D. Fcap. 8vo., cloth, 2s.

THINGS TO COME. A Prophetic Ode. By a well known Author. 8vo., sewed, 1s.

WHAT IS MESMERISM? Fcap. 8vo., sewed, 6d.

CHRIST AND THE CHURCH. 8vo., sewed, 9d.

THE DI

SPECT to EVIDENCE; or, The Peculiarities of the Latin Church evinced to be untenable on the Principles of Legitimate Historical Testimony. By GEORGE STANLEY FABER, B.D. Third Edition, revised and remoulded. 8vo., cloth, 10s. 6d.

THE ANATOMY OF POPERY.

CASES OF CONSCIENCE; for the use of the Laity. By PASCAL THE YOUNGER. Fourth Edition. 8vo., 2s. 6d.

"For powerful statements, startling facts, pungent wit, and that eloquence which is reasoning on fire, our day, fruitful in power, has produced nothing like 'Cases of Conscience.'"—*Archdeacon Garbett's Charge, August,* 1852.

AN EXPOSITION OF THE PRINCIPAL MOTIVES which induced ME to LEAVE the CHURCH of ROME. By C. L. TRIVIER, formerly a Roman Catholic Priest. Translated from the French by Mrs. Bushby. Fcap. 8vo., cloth, 3s. 6d.

"This little book, written by a man of the most extensive theological reading, is a compendium which we cannot too highly praise."—*Britannia.*

The POPE'S SUPREMACY a THING of PRIESTCRAFT; being a Compendious Refutation of the Arguments from Holy Scripture and Tradition, by which modern Romanists attempt to support the Papal Usurpation. By CHARLES HASTINGS COLLETTE, Author of "Romanism in England Exposed," &c. 8vo., containing 150 pages, 3s. 6d.

"The whole subject is examined with a minuteness and an accuracy which leave nothing to be accomplished in the way of proof."—*Bell's Weekly Messenger.*

LONDON: THOMAS BOSWORTH, 215, REGENT STREET.